D1544566

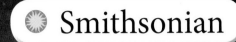

THE NATIONAL
AIR AND SPACE
MUSEUM

BY MEGAN COOLEY PETERSON

CAPSTONE PRESS
a capstone imprint

Smithsonian is published by Capstone Press,
1710 Roe Crest Drive, North Mankato, Minnesota 56003
www.mycapstone.com

Library of Congress Cataloging-in-Publication Data
Names: Peterson, Megan Cooley, author.
Title: The National Air and Space Museum / by Megan Cooley Peterson.
Description: North Mankato, Minnesota : Capstone Press, [2018] |
Series: Smithsonian field trips | Includes bibliographical references and index. |
Audience: Age 8–10 | Audience: Grades K to 3.
Identifiers: LCCN 2017011293| ISBN 9781515779742 (library binding) | ISBN 9781515779872 (pbk.)
| ISBN 9781515780052 (Ebook PDF)
Subjects: LCSH: National Air and Space Museum Juvenile literature.
Classification: LCC TL506.U6 W3764 2018 | DDC 629.1074/753—dc23
LC record available at https://lccn.loc.gov/2017011293

Editorial Credits
Michelle Hasselius, editor; Sarah Bennett, designer; Kelli Lageson, media researcher;
Laura Manthe, production specialist

Our very special thanks to Kealy Gordon, Product Development Manager; and Ellen Nanney, Licensing Manager,
Smithsonian, for their assistance. Capstone would also like to thank the following at Smithsonian Enterprises:
Brigid Ferraro, Vice President, Education and Consumer Products; Carol LeBlanc, Senior Vice President, Education,
and Consumer Products; and Christopher A. Liedel, President.

Photo Credits
©2017 National Air and Space Museum, Smithsonian: cover (all), 3, 4 (bottom), 6, 7 (all), 8 (bottom), 10,
12 (left and right), 13 (top right and bottom), 14, 16 (all), 17 (all), 18 (bottom), 19, 20, 23 (bottom left), 24, 25
(top right and bottom), 26, 28, (bottom); Alamy/John Frost Newspapers: 21 (top); Getty Images: Keystone-France/
Gamma-Keystone, 25 (top left); NASA Johnson Space Center: 8 (back), 9 (all), 13 (top left), 15 (top left and bottom
right), 22, 23 (top right and bottom right), 29 (right and bottom); National Archives and Records Administration:
27 (top); Newscom: Mondadori Portfolio, 27 (bottom), ZUMA Press/Keystone Pictures USA, 29 (top); Shutterstock:
David M. Schrader, 4 (design element, used throughout), Eugene Berman, 11 (bottom), Everett Historical, 28 (top),
kzww, 6 (design element, used throughout), Melissa Brandes, 21 (design element), nienora, 1 (design element,
used throughout), Pavel L Photo and Video, 4; XNR Productions, 21 (bottom)

Printed in the United States of America.
010399F17

Table of Contents

Soaring into the Future

The National Air and Space Museum is home to more than 60,000 objects. Each one tells a story about the people who pushed boundaries in space and aviation. It is one of the largest museums at the Smithsonian. Huge airplanes and spacecraft take up a lot of room. That's why the Museum has two buildings — one in Washington, D.C., and one in Chantilly, Virginia.

—Fact—

President Harry Truman signed a bill in 1946 that established the Museum. It was originally called the National Air Museum.

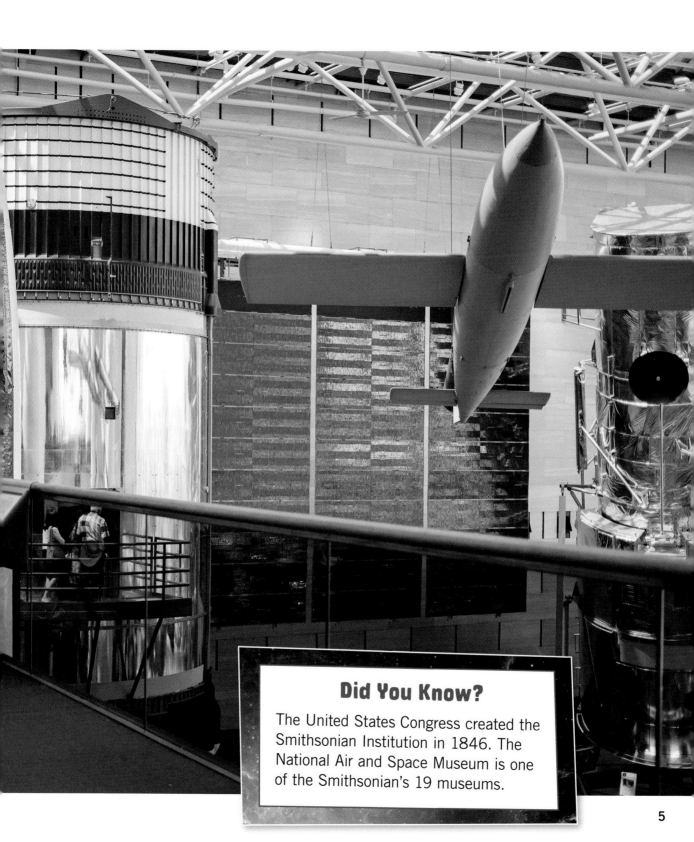

Did You Know?

The United States Congress created the Smithsonian Institution in 1846. The National Air and Space Museum is one of the Smithsonian's 19 museums.

Charles Lindbergh's *Spirit of St. Louis*

It took Charles Lindbergh 33 hours and 30 minutes to make aviation history. He boarded his plane, the *Spirit of St. Louis*, on May 20, 1927. Then Lindbergh flew nonstop from New York City to Paris, France. It was the first solo transatlantic flight between two major cities. Lindbergh donated the *Spirit of St. Louis* to the Smithsonian in 1928.

⬆ The *Spirit of St. Louis* is on display at the Air and Space Museum's *Boeing Milestones Flight Hall.*

⬇ On its trip back to the United States, the public couldn't see the famous plane up close. It was put on a U.S. Navy barge to prevent souvenir hunters.

⬇ the *Spirit of St. Louis* in 1927

⬆ the plane's cockpit

—Fact—
Lindbergh's historic flight covered 3,610 miles (5,810 kilometers).

Touchable Moon Rock

Have you ever wondered what the moon feels like? At the National Air and Space Museum, you can find out! The Museum has a slice of moon rock on display, and visitors can touch it. The rock slice is from a piece of volcanic rock called basalt. Astronauts from the Apollo 17 space mission collected the rock in 1972.

⬇ Visitors can touch the moon rock in the *Boeing Milestones of Flight Hall.*

—Fact—
The Smithsonian's Apollo 17 lunar touch rock is on loan from NASA.

Did You Know?

The Apollo 17 astronauts collected more than 740 moon rock and soil samples.

Lockheed U-2

The Lockheed U-2 was developed to gather intelligence from the Soviet Union during the Cold War (1946–1991). Flying at high altitudes, the aircraft took photographs more accurately than satellites. The Lockheed U-2C on display at the Smithsonian flew its first mission in 1956. Today other U-2 aircrafts continue to fly missions for the United States.

—Fact—

The Lockheed U-2 is nicknamed the "Dragon Lady."

Lockheed U-2 Stats

weight
13,071 pounds (5,929 kilograms)

wingspan
80 feet (24 meters)

length
50 feet (15 m)

height
15 feet (5 m)

Space Shuttle *Discovery*

The Space Shuttle *Discovery* was the third orbiter to fly in space. From 1984 to 2011, it circled Earth 39 times and spent 365 days in space. *Discovery* flew 184 men and women into space. It even deployed the Hubble Space Telescope.

⬇ the Space Shuttle *Discovery*

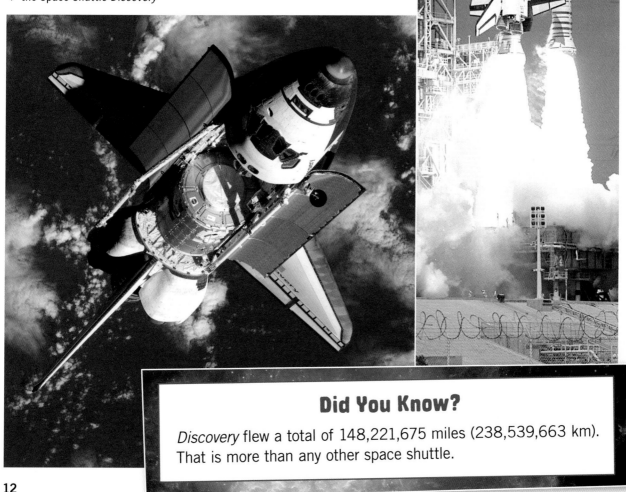

Did You Know?

Discovery flew a total of 148,221,675 miles (238,539,663 km). That is more than any other space shuttle.

Space Shuttle Program

NASA's Space Shuttle *Columbia* was the world's first space-rated space shuttle. The reusable spacecraft was launched on April 12, 1981. Four more shuttles followed — *Challenger*, *Discovery*, *Atlantis*, and *Endeavour*. These spacecraft flew a combined 135 missions. Astronauts on these shuttles launched and repaired satellites. They even helped build the International Space Station (ISS). The Space Shuttle program ended in 2011.

➡ *Discovery*'s final flight on February 24, 2011

⬆ astronauts C. Michael Foale (left) and Bernard A. Harris Jr. (right) exit *Discovery* to go on a spacewalk

➡ *Discovery* approaches the ISS in 2005

Broadcasting from Space

Lights, camera, action! The Museum has an RCA camera in its collection. But it's not just any camera.

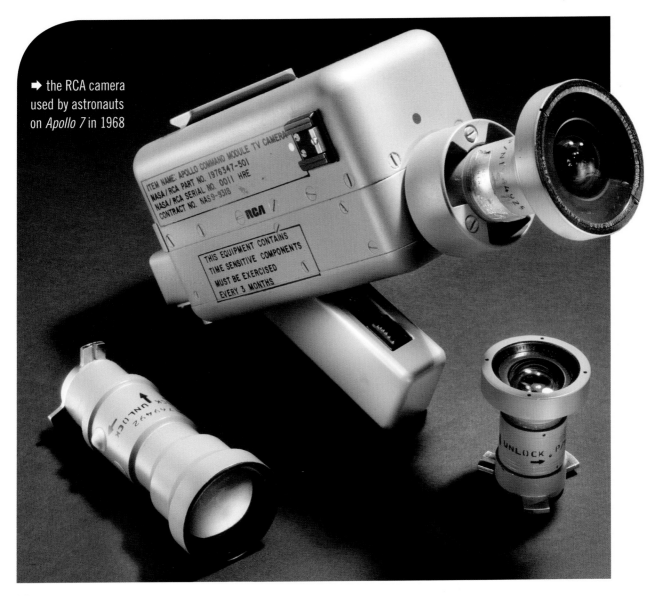

➡ the RCA camera used by astronauts on *Apollo 7* in 1968

Apollo 7 astronauts Don F. Eisele (left), Walter M. Schirra Jr. (center), and Walter Cunningham (right)

In October 1968 *Apollo 7* blasted into space. Astronauts orbited Earth 163 times during their 10-day mission. They filmed the first TV broadcast from space using the RCA camera. Viewers back on Earth watched the astronauts floating around in their spacecraft and catching objects. NASA gave the camera to the Smithsonian in 1972.

—Fact—

People on Earth saw the astronauts eat the first hot meal in space.

↑ *Apollo 7* launches into space

15

Spacey Spiders

Meet the eight-legged
astronauts, Anita and
Arabella! These female
cross spiders traveled
into space in May 1973.
Scientists wanted to see
if the spiders could spin
silk in zero gravity. The
59-day mission proved
spiders could spin webs
in weightlessness.

⬆ Anita the spider

⬅ a sample of Anita's web

16

Animals in Space

The first animals that the United States sent to space were fruit flies in 1949. In 1959 two female monkeys, Able and Baker, journeyed into space. The U.S. Army wanted to test the effects of space on living creatures. Both monkeys survived the journey. After Able died the monkey was donated to the National Air and Space Museum.

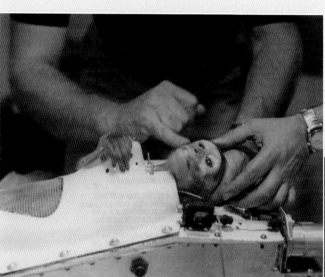

⬇ Able is part of the *Apollo to the Moon* exhibit at the Museum.

⬆ The monkeys had to lie inside biocapsules during their flight into space.

The 1903 Wright Flyer

On December 17, 1903, the Wright brothers gathered at the beach near Kitty Hawk, North Carolina. Wilbur and Orville Wright had spent four years perfecting their flying machine. It was made mostly of wood and fabric. Orville piloted the first successful flight of an engine-powered, heavier-than-air machine. He traveled 120 feet (36 m) in his historic 12-second flight. The Wright brothers paved the way for advances in aviation.

⬇ the Wright Flyer's first flight in 1903

"For some years I have been afflicted with the belief that flight is possible to man. My disease has increased in severity and I feel that it will soon cost me an increased amount of money if not my life.

I have been trying to arrange my affairs in such a way that I can devote my entire time for a few months to experiment in this field."

— *a letter written by Wilbur Wright in May 1900*

Early Milestones in Flight

1903
The Wright brothers make the first successful flight with a powered airplane.

1909
The Antoinette IV becomes the world's first successful monoplane.

1915
The Junkers J 1 is the world's first all-metal airplane.

Amelia Earhart's Lockheed Vega

Legendary pilot Amelia Earhart set two records in her Lockheed Vega 5B. She was the first woman to fly solo nonstop across the Atlantic Ocean and the first to fly across the United States. She made her historic flights in 1932. Earhart's Lockheed Vega came to the Smithsonian in 1966.

—Fact—
Earhart traveled 2,447 miles (3,938 km) in her flight across the United States.

➡ Earhart named her red plane the "Little Red Bus." It is on display in the *Pioneers of Flight* gallery.

AMELIA EARHART MISSING IN PACIFIC

★ ★ Home

RED LINE

Herald and Examiner

Chicago

BAN RIOT FILM IN CHICAGO

COMPLETE SPORTS

Two Sections—Part 1—THREE CENTS

VOL. LVII—NO. 63 C9 MONDAY—JULY 5—1937

HEAR AMELIA'S FAINT CALLS

PIRATES 7, CUBS 6
SECOND GAME

RUSH POLICE TO S. CHICAGO STRIKE AREA

ANNOUNCEMENT

Los Angeles, Calif., July 3, 1937.

Editor The Herald and Examiner, Chicago, Ill.

Please stop in their tracks hostile rumors being circulated in Chicago.

The Herald and Examiner will not be consolidated with any other paper.

It will not be changed in style, character or form.

...continue to be published

...se, not for sale.

W. R. HEARST.

Searchers' Hopes Revived by Signals; 57 Planes on Way

Speeded to Aid by Carrier;
Destroyers Join Hunt

SOX 9, BROWNS

25c

WANT ADS

A Smile for Calcutta

What Happened to Amelia?

In 1937 Amelia Earhart attempted to fly around the world in her Lockheed Electra 10-E Special airplane. Earhart and her navigator Fred Noonan left California on May 20. On July 2, the U.S. Navy picked up Earhart's final radio signals. She was out of fuel. The U.S. Navy and Coast Guard launched a search. It was the most massive and expensive search in U.S. history. No one saw or heard from her again. Earhart's plane has never been found. Many believe she crashed into the Pacific Ocean. No one knows how she died.

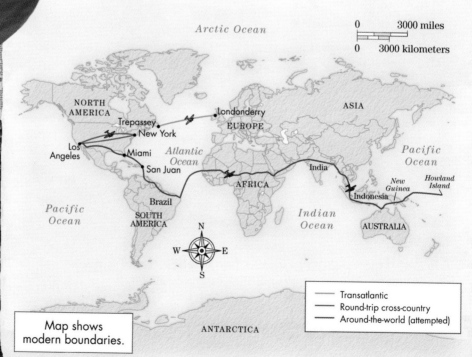

Map shows modern boundaries.

Legend:
— Transatlantic
— Round-trip cross-country
— Around-the-world (attempted)

21

Apollo 13 Vest

In April 1970 the crew aboard *Apollo 13* was in trouble. They were supposed to land on the moon. But one of two oxygen tanks on board exploded. Then the second tank failed. As the aircraft circled the moon, it lost power. The crew was running out of water. The cabin lost heat.

"Houston, we've had a problem here."

— Astronaut Jack Swigert to mission control in Houston, Texas.

Back on Earth, mission control flight director Gene Kranz jumped into action. For days he and his team worked around the clock to find a way to save the crew. Kranz, wearing a white vest, guided the astronauts safely home. In 2006 he donated his vest to the Smithsonian.

⬆ Kranz watches the *Apollo 13* crew on the screen from mission control on April 13, 1970. Shortly after the broadcast, the aircraft's oxygen tank exploded.

⬆ *Apollo 13* astronauts Fred Haise Jr. (left), James Lovell Jr. (center), and John Swigert Jr. (right)

⬇ Gene Kranz (left) and the rest of mission control watch as *Apollo 13* returns to Earth

—Fact—

Martha Kranz, Gene's wife, sewed his famous vest.

World's First Pressure Suit

The Museum has one of the world's first pressure suits on display. In March 1935 pilot Wiley Post flew from California to Ohio. At times his Lockheed Vega reached heights of more than 30,000 feet (9,144 m). At that height the air is very thin. There wasn't much oxygen, and his cabin wasn't pressurized. To solve this problem, Post wore a pressure suit. The suit provided the oxygen and air pressure he needed to survive. Post could fly longer distances at higher altitudes. The suit led to the development of modern spacesuits.

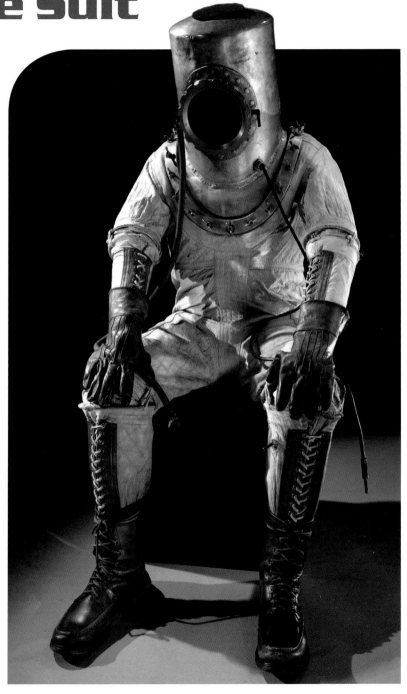

—Fact—
The B.F. Goodrich company created Post's pressure suit.

⬇ When the suit was pressurized, Post could not bend his arms or legs.

Did You Know?

⬅ Wiley Post made the first solo flight around the world in 1933. Post's plane, the *Winnie Mae*, is also on display at the Smithsonian.

WINNIE MAE

NR-105W

Captured Zero Fighter

In April 1944 the U.S. captured 12 Japanese aircraft on Saipan Island. The Zero Fighter featured at the Smithsonian is believed to be one of them.

⬆ The Mitsubishi A6M5 Reisen (Zero Fighter) aircraft is on display in the *World War II Aviation* exhibit.

—Fact—

The Japanese built more than 10,000 Zero Fighters.

The Imperial Japanese Navy used the Zero Fighter during World War II (1939–1945). This fighter plane was one of Japan's most feared weapons. It could reach speeds of more than 330 miles (531 km) per hour. The Zero could outmaneuver and fly farther than other fighter planes.

↓ a Zero Fighter takes off from a Japanese aircraft carrier to join the attack on Pearl Harbor on December 7, 1941

Did You Know?

The Zero Fighter is also called the Mitsubishi A6M5 Reisen. In Japanese, reisen means "zero fighter."

PT 109

↑ a Zero Fighter drops a bomb near Munson Island, Florida, in the film *PT-109* in 1963

Mobile Quarantine Facility

On July 20, 1969, Apollo 11 astronauts stepped onto the moon. It was the world's first moon landing. The astronauts brought back moon rocks, moon dust . . . and moon germs? Scientists worried the astronauts might have brought back unknown germs or diseases from space. So the men were kept in NASA's Mobile Quarantine Facility for 88 hours. The facility was flown to the Johnson Space Center in Houston, Texas. The astronauts were still inside during the flight. NASA gave the Mobile Quarantine Facility to the Smithsonian in 1974.

→ Apollo 11 astronauts enter the quarantine trailer on July 24, 1969

← inside the Mobile Quarantine Facility

Glossary

altitude (AL-ti-tood)—how high a place is above sea level or Earth's surface

aviation (ay-ve-AY-shuhn)—the science of building and flying aircraft

broadcast (BRAHD-kast)—a program on TV

gravity (GRAV-uh-tee)—a force that pulls objects with mass together; gravity pulls objects down toward the center of Earth

intelligence (in-TEL-uh-jenss)—information secretly gathered by spies or electronic devices about an enemy's plans or actions

International Space Station (in-tur-NASH-uh-nuhl SPAYSS STAY-shuhn)—a place for astronauts to live and work in space

legendary (LEJ-uhnd-air-ee)—something or someone that is well-known or famous

monoplane (mon-oh-PLAYN)—an airplane with one pair of wings

orbiter (OR-bit-ur)—the main part of a space shuttle; the orbiter is the part of the shuttle that goes into space and returns to Earth

outmaneuver (OUT-muh-noo-ver)—to get away from someone or something by moving faster or with greater agility

pressurize (PRESH-uh-rize)—to seal off an area so that the air pressure inside is the same as at Earth's surface

quarantine (KWOR-uhn-teen)—the act of keeping something separate from a larger group

satellite (SAT-uh-lite)—a spacecraft that circles Earth; satellites gather and send information

transatlantic (tran-suht-LAN-tik)—crossing the Atlantic Ocean

Read More

Graham, Ian. *You Wouldn't Want to Be on Apollo 13!: A Mission You'd Rather Not Go On.* You Wouldn't Want To. New York: Franklin Watts, 2017.

Lassieur, Allison. *International Space Station: An Interactive Space Exploration Adventure.* You Choose: Space. North Mankato, Minn.: Capstone Press, 2017.

McAneney, Caitlin. *The First Solo Flight Across the Atlantic.* Incredible True Adventures. New York: Gareth Stevens Publishing, 2015.

Critical Thinking Questions

1. Amelia Earhart set two records in her Lockheed Vega 5B. What were they?

2. Wiley Post wore one of the first pressurized suits in 1935. What does "pressurized" mean?

3. Why were the Apollo 11 astronauts quarantined after they returned from the moon? Are astronauts still quarantined today?

Internet Sites

Use FactHound to find Internet sites related to this book.

Visit *www.facthound.com*

Just type in 9781515779742 and go.

Check out projects, games and lots more at
www.capstonekids.com

Index